IRELAND

By Sloane Gould and
Ann Poeschel

EXPLORING
WORLD
CULTURES

Cavendish
Square

Published in 2024 by Cavendish Square Publishing, LLC
2544 Clinton Street, Buffalo, NY 14224

Second Edition

Library of Congress Cataloging-in-Publication Data

Names: Gould, Sloane, author. | Poeschel, Ann, author.
Title: Ireland / Sloane Gould and Ann Poeschel.
Description: Buffalo, NY : Cavendish Square Publishing, [2024] | Series: Exploring world cultures | "First edition by Ann Poeschel. Second edition by Sloane Gould." | Includes bibliographical references and index.
Identifiers: LCCN 2023011134 (print) | LCCN 2023011135 (ebook) | ISBN 9781502667618 (library binding) | ISBN 9781502667601 (paperback) | ISBN 9781502667625 (ebook)
Subjects: LCSH: Ireland--Juvenile literature.
Classification: LCC DA906 .G68 2024 (print) | LCC DA906 (ebook) | DDC 914.1504--dc23/eng/20230310
LC record available at https://lccn.loc.gov/2023011134
LC ebook record available at https://lccn.loc.gov/2023011135

Writers: Ann Poeschel; Sloane Gould (second edition)
Editor: Caitie McAneney
Copyeditor: Shannon Harts
Designer: Andrea Davison-Bartolotta

The photographs in this book are used by permission and through the courtesy of: Cover Lapina/Shutterstock.com; p. 4 MNStudio/Shutterstock.com; p. 5 Atomazul/Shutterstock.com; p. 6 Maria_Janus/Shutterstock.com; p. 7 Fabiano's_Photo/Shutterstock.com; p. 8 National Library of Ireland/Flickr; p. 9 Everett Collection/Shutterstock.com; p. 10 Semmick Photo/Shutterstock.com; p. 11 brichuas/Shutterstock.com; p. 13 (top) Benny Marty/Shutterstock.com; p. 13 (bottom) Piotr Orlinski/Shutterstock.com; p. 15 (top) Richard Semik/Shutterstock.com; p. 15 (bottom) grafxart/Shutterstock.com; p. 16 Leonid Andronov/Shutterstock.com; p. 17 Irene Fox/Shutterstock.com; p. 18 Daniel M. Nagy/Shutterstock.com; p. 19 EyesTravelling/Shutterstock.com; p. 20 M Reel/Shutterstock.com; p. 21 Fominayaphoto/Shutterstock.com; p. 22 mark gusev/Shutterstock.com; p. 23 Lukassek/Shutterstock.com; p. 24 Cenz07/Shutterstock.com; p. 25 DarkBird/Shutterstock.com; p. 26 Hristo Anestev/Shutterstock.com; p. 27 D. Ribeiro/Shutterstock.com; p. 28 Robyn Mackenzie/Shutterstock.com; p. 29 Brent Hofacker/Shutterstock.com.

CPSIA compliance information: Batch #CS24CSQ: For further information contact Cavendish Square Publishing LLC at 1-877-980-4450.

Printed in the United States of America

CONTENTS

INTRODUCTION

Ireland is a green country known for its special music, writing, and dancing. The Republic of Ireland is an independent country. It's part of the European Union, a partnership of more than two dozen countries in Europe.

This island nation is in western Europe. It had a tough history, including unfair treatment by England and **famine**. However, Ireland's history also includes

Newgrange is an ancient monument, or building, made in Ireland more than 5,000 years ago.

amazing artwork and buildings from ancient, or very old, **civilizations**. For hundreds of years, Irish people have been known as great storytellers, and many classical books came from Ireland.

Ireland has beautiful views that include rocky coastlines overlooking the Atlantic Ocean. It also has sandy beaches, busy cities and towns, and many farms. Walking, biking, and surfing are all great ways to explore nature in Ireland. Today, it's a wonderful place to visit and enjoy the rich landscape and **culture**.

Ireland has many colorful coastal towns.

GEOGRAPHY

Ireland has a **diverse** landscape. Surrounded by the Atlantic Ocean, this island is divided into two parts. Much of it is the Republic of Ireland. The northeastern part is called Northern Ireland, which is part of the United Kingdom.

BOGS

Peat bogs, found in western Ireland, are remains of ancient lakes that dried up. People have burned peat for fuel for hundreds of years.

The Burren in western Ireland is a wide area of limestone rock.

Much of Ireland is farmland.

Ireland's nickname is "the Emerald Isle." That's because it's so green there. It has grassy plains, mountains, and coastlines. It has many lakes and rivers. The longest river is called the River Shannon. One famous feature is the Cliffs of Moher—high cliff faces formed hundreds of millions of years ago.

The weather in Ireland is usually not very hot or cold, but mostly in the middle. It rains a lot in Ireland! That's why the grass and trees are so green.

HISTORY

People have lived in Ireland for more than 8,000 years. As early as 5000 BCE, Celts from central Europe arrived. They were pagan, or believed in many gods. However, in 432 CE, a man who became known as St. Patrick arrived and taught the people about Christianity.

This picture shows Dublin after the Easter Uprising in 1916.

Ireland became part of the United Kingdom 1801. The British treated the Irish unfairly, especially Catholics—people who followed the Roman Catholic branch of the Christian faith. Irish Catholics couldn't own land. In the 1840s, the Irish potato crop had a sickness. During this time, millions of people died of hunger or left Ireland.

FACT!
In 1949, the Republic of Ireland became completely independent.

On Easter Monday 1916, some Irish people started an uprising for independence, which sparked a war. In 1922, the Irish Free State was founded, while Northern Ireland stayed part of the United Kingdom.

The Potato Famine of the 1840s is also called the Great Famine.

VIKINGS

In the 800s, Vikings arrived in Ireland. They fought with the Celts for hundreds of years.

GOVERNMENT

The Republic of Ireland allows people to vote for their **representatives** in government. The National **Parliament,** called the Oireachtas (irr-OCK-tuss), meets in the capital city of Dublin. The National Parliament consists of the president and two houses of parliament.

FACT!

The constitution, or set of laws, of Ireland went into effect in 1937.

The Irish flag is green, white, and orange.

The president is the head of state and the armed forces. They oversee the work of the two houses of parliament. The houses of parliament are called Dáil Éireann (DAWL EHR-in) and Seanad Éireann (SHAN-uhd EHR-in). Dáil Éireann is led by the prime minister, called the taoiseach (TEE-shock). The taoiseach leads the government. The Supreme Court and lower courts uphold the law.

MAJOR CITIES

People live in both cities and in the country in Ireland. The most populated cities are Dublin, Cork, Limerick, and Galway.

The Republic of Ireland has 26 counties, or parts. Northern Ireland has six.

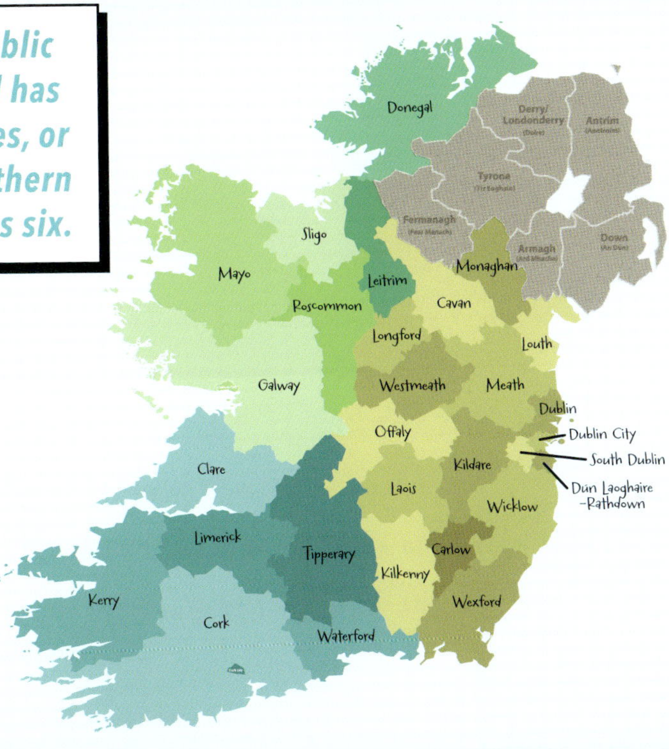

THE ECONOMY

Ireland's **economy** was based around farming for thousands of years. The Industrial Revolution brought many factories in the 1800s. Then, in the 1990s and 2000s, new businesses, or industries, took root, and the economy grew. Today, Ireland has many different industries. Technology, medicine, food, and tourism help make Ireland successful.

FACT!

During its economic boom in the 1990s and 2000s, Ireland was known as the "Celtic Tiger."

The Republic of Ireland is a popular place for businesses. Dublin and Cork are important cities for technology. Companies such as Apple, Facebook, and Google have their European headquarters, or bases, in Ireland.

GROWING QUICKLY

Ireland sells goods to other countries to keep its economy healthy. It has the fastest-growing economy in the European Union as of 2023.

Tourism, or people visiting from other countries, is also important. In 2015, Irish-based Ryanair became the first airline to carry more than 100 million international passengers in a single year.

Ireland uses the euro for money. Its coins have a harp on them.

Many Irish tourists enjoy the Cliffs of Moher.

THE ENVIRONMENT

Ireland is known for its beautiful natural environment, or surroundings. Many animals and plants live in Ireland. The waters surrounding Ireland are home to a large dolphin, whale, and seal population.

Irish people value a clean and healthy environment. They have some of the best air, water, and soil in Europe. The country tries to take care of the environment. One way leaders do this is by encouraging people to ride their bikes. In Dublin, enough people walk or bike each day to take 330,000 cars off the road.

Many Irish people use different kinds of energy to get electricity. Waterpower and wind power are two of the most common green, or environmentally-friendly, energy sources.

ENVIRONMENTAL ISSUES

Pollution is a concern in Ireland. Cars and farming produce harmful gases, which can hurt the environment.

This seal rests on a rock in Bantry Bay.

FACT!

Warmer weather due to climate change could harm Ireland's environment.

Much of Ireland is pasture, or a space for cows and sheep to eat.

THE PEOPLE TODAY

Today, just over 5 million people live in Ireland. Many people living in Ireland have proud Irish roots. They can trace their families back for many years in Ireland. However, many **immigrants** are also arriving in the country. Some have come from Poland, Latvia, and the Czech Republic. Immigrants bring new cultures to the country and help make Ireland a more diverse place.

About 1.5 million people live in Dublin.

Many people in other countries have Irish **ancestors**. In the 1800s and early 1900s, around 4.5 million Irish people traveled to the United States. Many Americans are proud of their Irish heritage, or roots.

A community called the Irish Travellers is a **minority** in Ireland. They have their own unique heritage, practices, and languages.

FACT!

Many Irish Travellers live in cities in large family groups.

These Irish kids play in snow in Dublin.

COUNTRY VS. CITY

Most people in Ireland live in cities. However, Ireland has one of the most rural, or country-living, populations in the European Union.

LIFESTYLE

Irish people value family and community. Some families are quite large. Irish Travellers tend to have more children per family than the general population. Irish people are proud of their heritage. The "O" in Irish names like O'Brien means "descended from." It lets people know someone has Irish heritage.

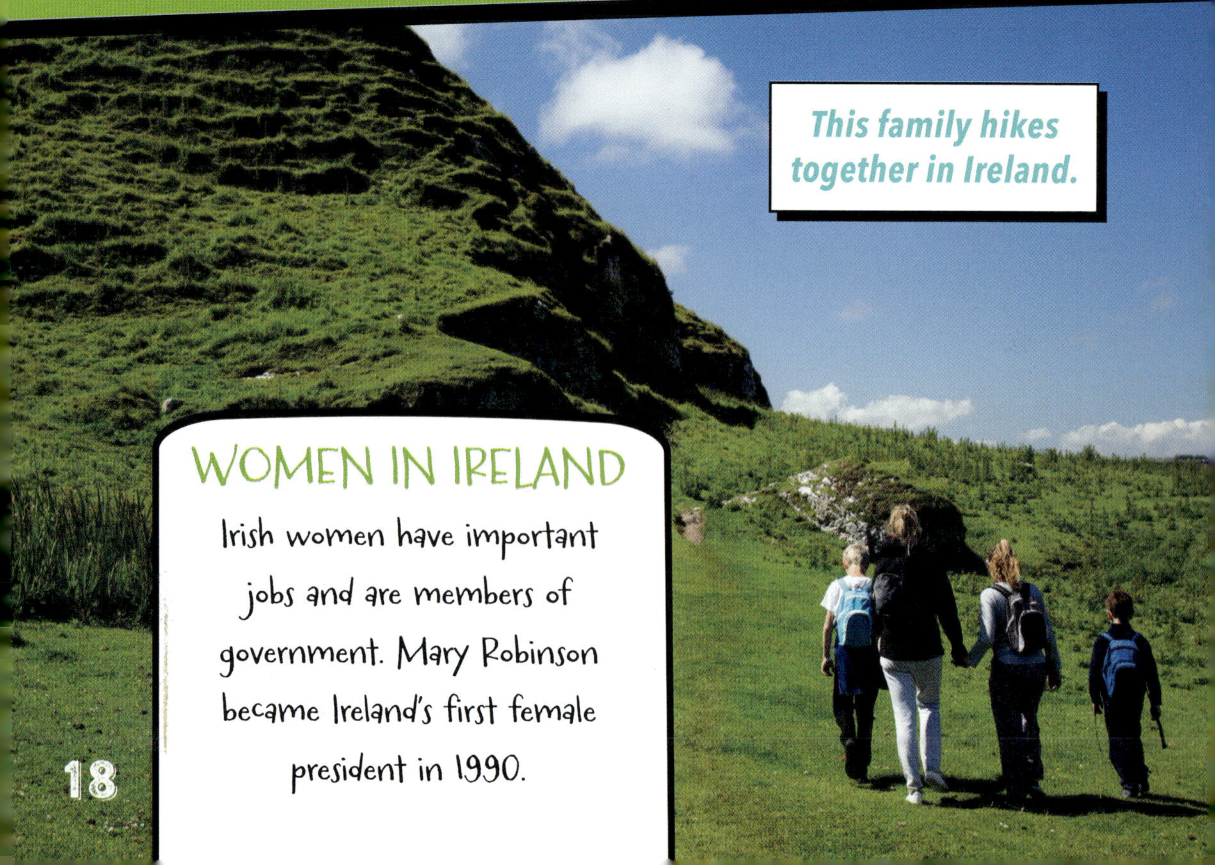

This family hikes together in Ireland.

WOMEN IN IRELAND

Irish women have important jobs and are members of government. Mary Robinson became Ireland's first female president in 1990.

Irish children start school young. When older, many young adults will go on to a university or college. Major colleges in Ireland include Trinity College in Dublin and University College Cork in County Cork.

People living in cities such as Dublin, Cork, and Limerick travel on buses or trains, and by biking or walking. Many people use cars to get around the country. They use ferries to travel to smaller islands and to Great Britain.

FACT!

Some Irish people live in small communities on islands. The Aran Islands are off the coast of Galway.

This is a small Aran Island community.

RELIGION

Christianity has been the main Irish religion, or belief system, for hundreds of years, since it was brought to Ireland by St. Patrick. Catholics were treated badly under British rule, but the Catholic Church greatly shaped Irish society after Ireland gained its independence. One of the most beautiful copies of the part of the Bible (the Christian holy book) called the Gospels is in Dublin. It is called the Book of Kells.

About 78 percent of people in the Republic of Ireland are Roman Catholic, while 3 percent are Anglican (a kind of Protestant Christian). Violence, or fighting, between Catholics and Protestants has happened in Ireland over the years.

Shamrocks are a symbol, or sign, of Ireland because of St. Patrick.

Not all Irish people are Christians. The largest non-Christian religion is Islam. Today, about 10 percent of Irish people have no religion at all.

FACT!

Ireland has no official state religion, though most schools are run by the Catholic Church.

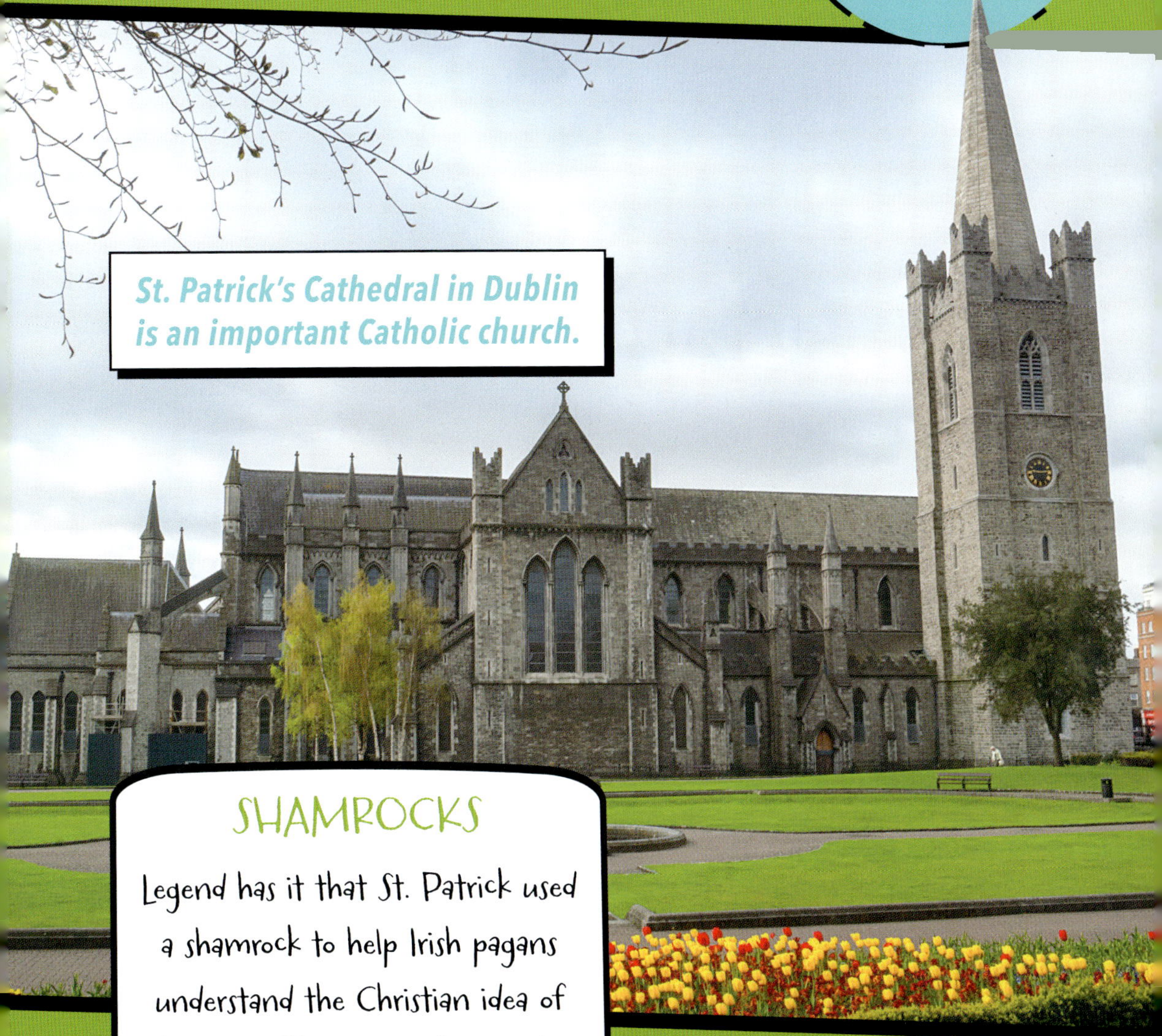

St. Patrick's Cathedral in Dublin is an important Catholic church.

SHAMROCKS

Legend has it that St. Patrick used a shamrock to help Irish pagans understand the Christian idea of the "Holy Trinity," or that God is the father, son, and Holy Spirit.

LANGUAGE

Nearly everyone in Ireland speaks English. However, many also speak the native language, Gaelic (also called Irish). Street signs and place names are written in both languages. Laws are also written in both. All students must study Irish in school.

FACT!
Irish and English are the official languages of the Republic of Ireland.

"Fáilte" means "welcome."

Irish is one of the oldest written languages. An alphabet called the Ogham alphabet was used to write the early Irish language. It is made up of lines often carved into stone. You can find parts of these carvings around Ireland.

The Gaeltacht (gail-TOCHT) describes places where most of the population speaks Irish. The Gaeltacht includes parts of counties Donegal, Galway, Kerry, and Mayo.

OTHER LANGUAGES

Because more immigrants are moving to Ireland, many other languages are arriving too. Polish and French are common.

This Gaeltacht sign tells people they're in an Irish-speaking area.

ARTS AND FESTIVALS

Irish people love to celebrate and have fun. Dancing and music are important in Ireland. **Traditional** Irish dancing is taught in schools. People dance at gatherings called *céilís* (CAY-lees). Ireland is famous for Riverdance, a popular performance featuring Irish dancers.

FACT!

Arts and music festivals include the Galway Arts Festival in Galway (July) and the Temple Bar TradFest in Dublin (January).

This statue in Sligo, Ireland, shows famous poet William Butler Yeats.

LITERATURE

Ireland is known for its literature, or writings. Famous authors include James Joyce, Oscar Wilde, and William Butler Yeats.

Musicians often gather to play traditional Irish music. They use instruments such as the bodhrán (BOW-rawn) drum, uilleann (ILL-yin) pipes, tin whistle, and fiddle. Ireland has many arts festivals, music festivals, and other outdoor events. St. Patrick's Festival in March is one of the largest celebrations of the year. Everyone gets the day off, and there are parades all over the country. Halloween began in Ireland as the Samhain (sow-IHN) celebration. It is the country's oldest festival.

Irish dancers pose in their costumes.

FUN AND PLAY

Ireland has many popular sports and activities. The Gaelic Athletic Association (GAA) organizes the national games of Ireland. The major Irish games include hurling, camogie, and Gaelic football. These games have been around for centuries, with ties back to the ancient Celts. They are loved by children and adults.

FACT!

Other popular sports include soccer, rugby, cycling, and rowing.

People surf at Inch Beach in County Kerry, Ireland.

Irish people enjoy outdoor activities when the weather is nice. There are many beautiful beaches where people like to walk and surf. The water is cold, but Ireland has some great waves!

Many cities offer museums and art galleries. People also like to stroll around and listen to people play music in pubs and on the street.

HURLING AND CAMOGIE

Hurling is an ancient sport. Players use a wooden stick called a hurley to hit a small ball. Women play a similar sport called camogie.

Gaelic football is a popular Irish sport.

FOOD

Ireland is famous for its hearty meals of meat and potatoes. Examples of these meals are Irish stew, meat pie and potatoes, and "bangers and mash" (sausage and mashed potatoes).

Tea is an important part of Irish culture. People drink it several times a day. Having a cup of tea is called having a "cuppa." It is served at every meal and enjoyed by people of all ages.

Irish stew is often made with lamb.

Ireland has many pubs where people gather to eat, drink, and talk. Pubs are local meeting places for sharing good times with friends and family. Many pubs offer meals, snacks, and live music. Getting together to eat and drink is just one way that Irish culture has lived on for thousands of years.

FACT!

Soda bread is a traditional Irish bread sometimes eaten with seeds, honey, or dried fruit.

Families often have special recipes for soda bread.

TIME FOR BREAKFAST!

A traditional "full Irish breakfast" includes eggs, breads, tea, and meats such as bacon and black and white puddings (sausages).

GLOSSARY

ancestors: Family members from whom a person has descended.

civilization: An organized society with written records and laws.

climate change: Change in Earth's climate, or long-term weather patterns, caused by human activity.

culture: The beliefs and ways of life of a certain group of people.

diverse: Including many different parts.

economy: The way things are made, sold, and used in a country or area.

famine: A problem in which many people do not have enough to eat.

immigrant: A person who comes to a country to live there.

minority: A group of people who are different from the larger group in a country or other area in some way.

parliament: A lawmaking body.

peat: Brown earthy material found in bogs and used for fuel or in garden soil.

representative: A person who stands or acts for others.

traditional: Something that has been done for a long time.

FIND OUT MORE

Books

O'Brien Jr., John. *Celebrating St. Patrick's Day: History, Traditions, and Activities*. Emeryville, CA: Rockridge Press, 2021.

Roberts, Jack L. *A Kid's Guide to Ireland*. Curious Kids Press, 2022.

Website

Ireland Facts: All About the Emerald Isle!
www.natgeokids.com/uk/discover/geography/countries/facts-about-ireland/
Explore more fun facts about Ireland with *National Geographic Kids*.

Video

Destination Ireland
www.youtube.com/watch?v=bQwdahZwe0M
Enjoy this tour through Ireland with *National Geographic*.

INDEX